# DELIVERED

HATTIE LAWS

Emerge Publishing Group, LLC
Riviera Beach, FL
www.emergepublishers.com

Library of Congress Control Number 2009939660

ISBN 978-0-9825699-0-0

Published by
Emerge Publishing Group, LLC
Riviera Beach, FL
www.emergepublishers.com

Cover Art and Design by Gloria

Hattie Laws, 2009
Delivered! / Hattie Laws
1. Christianity.  2. Autobiography.


Printed in the United States of America

# SPECIAL THANKS TO:

*Pastor Gregory Washington and his
lovely wife and companion, Carla Washington;
My non-compromising friend and
father in Christ, Pastor Elder John H. Lawson;
My sister through it all, De Angela Butler
(I love you girl); Elder and Sister Evans.*

*My deepest gratitude for
your assistance, your continuous
encouragements and most of
all your faithful prayers.*

# CONTENTS

# P R E F A C E

I often look back at my past, "wondering how I got over". Now, I only look forward with the thoughts of knowing I no longer have to be ashamed of my past or it having a hold on me.

I'm now using my past as a stepping stone to fulfil my purpose, goals here on earth and preparing for the after. If asked, what motivated me to change or live my life in a positive way, I'd say, "my death".

During my drug use, my biggest desire was to die and free everyone of my presence. Yet, it wasn't until the day that I died (February 23, 2004) that I started to live again.

# Chapter 1

## *Starting Out*

I won't start at the first year of my 17 years of drug abuse. I couldn't remember it if I tried. I will try to start somewhere in my life at the age of 21 years old.

I had my 2 year old daughter living with me, even though I was told during my pregnancy by my parents that they would adopt and raise the child if I agreed not to have an abortion (only if the child was a girl). The agreement lasted about a month. My parents were still busy partying. They required a babysitter. Who better for the job than me, the mother. This led the baby girl back to me. I was angry but I took her back.

I lived in a newly built two-bedroom apartment. The unit was in a two-story duplex in a very nice neighborhood, across from a golf-course. The neighborhood's amenities didn't seem to make a difference because all of the tenants, including myself, were from the old projects.

Yet, I thought myself and my daughter to be a better caliber of 'project material'. I even had standards. For instance, I didn't borrow food from the neighbors. I didn't sit outside with them and gossip. I didn't leave my door open for unwanted visits. I didn't bum cigarettes, so they wouldn't bum off me. I never asked anyone to watch my daughter because I knew there was no way I would watch their children.

Two years after moving into the duplex, I was still there. My daughter was growing up and needed to interact with others that weren't from where we lived. I allowed her outside for an hour each day but only on the back side of the apartment. I didn't want anyone to see us. "Why all the hiding?" I asked myself at times. My answer was, "Because you're just like the other tenants. No husband means no respect."

# CHAPTER 2

## *Stumbling Block*

I've learned that living as a Black woman means that your goals and dreams can be a problem for other people. Even family. You'd think that family would understand, that they'd be there. Not so. Family will gut you. They will be the first to gut you.

I was doing motel work to pay my bills as well as support my daughter. After work, I wanted to go out and party with my friends. My mother would say, "You must not have worked hard enough. If you had, you'd be too tired to go out." "I'm 21 not 40," I'd say. If I were running late the next day (even a

minute late) she'd drive right past my house. She
didn't wait. She didn't call. Nothing. Her response
for leaving me was "If you had stayed home last
night you'd be on time." Honestly, I felt she just
didn't want me working where she was. She used to
tell me how her floor was always selected as the
cleanest of all the eight floors at the motel and how
she was "employee of the month" every month until
I began working there. Now, she had to split
everything with me. Management couldn't decide
who to give "employee of the month" to. She often
told me to find something else to do. I was cutting
hers short.

This is family, my mother, the same one that
would ride right past me as I sat by the road waiting
on her. There were days that the rain would be
pouring so hard I couldn't see my hand in front of my
face. She'd call ahead to tell me, "You'd better be
ready." She didn't show up.

I'd had quite enough. I no longer cared to work
with my mother. Don't misjudge me. I love my
mother. I always have. I often thought it was she
who didn't love me. Yes, I often resented things that
were said or done in our house when I was growing
up. Maybe that's the reason some of my choices
caused me to make the wrong decisions. Decisions
that I often thought were the best decisions.

No longer working with my mother led to not working at all. This didn't stop her from doing what she was doing. She would say, "You need a job to pay your bills. There's no room at my house for y'all." Trust me, I had no intention of going back to her house. Let's not get it twisted. I'd quit my job. I hadn't quit being a mother (at least not at the moment).

I had rent, utilities, phone bills, gas bills, and a daughter to feed and clothe. I had to do something to make sure she got what she needed. I had never once been late with my rent. Now, I had to tell my landlord that I'd quit my job. What could I have been thinking? Well, I didn't have to think too long of a way to tell her I'd quit. Remember, I lived in a housing duplex. The other single mothers had done my bidding for me. They'd done such a great job of relaying the information, in fact, that she was at my door the next morning, inquiring about how I intended to pay next month's rent.

During the two years that I lived there, I recalled three other residents who held a job for a year or two: the landlord; a single mother across the walk from me, and myself. The others worked out of their apartments, 'at night'. These 'night workers' always had continuous traffic and movement between the hours of 11:30pm - 4:00am. I watched these things take place, taking mental notes. After losing my job I began to think - "I might have to start getting it just like the rest of them. Quick - late at night." (Just a thought, for right now, anyway).

# CHAPTER 3

## *Up Again*

I can recall the morning I chose to go job hunting. I decided to use my front door that particular morning. I didn't want to mess my heels up with the wet sand at my back door. I dressed my daughter in her prettiest dress, braided her hair, applied matching barrettes, ruffled socks, and patent leather shoes. This ought to make grandmas and granddad babysit (if only for an hour or long enough for me to do what I needed to do). As we prepared to leave, I double checked the door (mind you, I was still paying on my furniture). As I look up, it was as though the entire complex had a monitor on my front door and they had all been alerted that I was on my way out.

I promise, there were nine apartments total, and the eight other mothers were outside, standing in their doorways, sitting on the stairs, leaning on their balconies. All watching as I towed my daughter down the sidewalk. I never talked to any of these women and they weren't speaking to me this morning. They just glared and gawked as I walked down the center sidewalk. In response to their gazes, I stood a little taller and held my head a little higher. When I turned the corner out of earshot and away from glaring eyes, I relaxed. I realized I had strained my neck. I must have stretched it further than what the Lord allowed.

Well, dressing my daughter up worked. The grandparents agreed to keep her and I set out to go job hunting.

I haven't described to you the place where I live: It's a one horse, one traffic light town, called New Smyrna Beach. It's known for its beach and downtown historical area. If you can't pronounce it, I'll break it down for you - N.S.B. That's it. N.S.B has a Seven Eleven, two elementary schools, one middle school, and one high school. Our mall, as I've heard it called, is the WalMart plaza. Other shopping options are Kmart and Goodyear, where one could order from the Sears catalog. There were four locations where the folks congregated during the week and on weekends to drink, party and hook up. There used to be a joint named 'Hommy's Place'. It was open on Wednesday and Sunday from 11pm until 2am. Hommy's was licensed to sell liquor and beer as well as food. It sat 10 people comfortably - but if the D.J. played "No Parking on the Dance Floor," it held 50 people all night long. I don't know if it was because of how old and worn down this place was that the walls expanded at times or because of how hot it was inside that the sweat allowed us to slide against each other. The food Hommy's sold was fish only. If you planned to go bar hopping, your best bet would be to go to Hommy's last. The smell of old fried fish grease was so strong that it took two days to lose the scent from your hair - a week if you dared to enter.

The second place was called Ebony & Ivory. This establishment was divided in half. That means the building had whites in the front and blacks in the back. This was the rule:

*"No Blacks at no time shall be, nor will be served upon entering through the front door. You must enter at the back of this building in order to place an order or purchase any packaged liquor."*

I remember asking the owner, Mary Anne, one day after drinking a half pint of gin, what she would do if I came through the front. She answered, "I'll have your black ass locked up." She then asked me if I needed anymore ice to go with my drink, before walking away from the window. We were treated like "niggers" because we allowed her to treat us as such. Ebony & Ivory was a place I could go to shoot pool, talk some trash, dance to the jukebox, and flirt with men (young and especially old). It didn't take anything to buy a tube top and multi-colored shirt. I put the tube top on as a skirt, donned the multi-colored shirt and a pair of matching pumps. My parents babysat my daughter while I went to Ebony & Ivory on a Friday to shoot pool and while I seriously looked for a job.

The other place in town was "*Soft As Silk*". The younger crowd (20 - 40 yrs. old) frequented here. Soft as Silk opened at 8am and stayed open all day, every day. Rain, sleet, or snow - every day of the week - Soft as Silk was guaranteed at least 3-4 shootings, 3 stabbings, and 1 overdose. A "shake 'em down" happened every Saturday by N.S.B.'s finest. The older crowd refused to come, even on oldies but goodies night.

Then there was the Down & Dirty BBQ Restaurant. This place was located in the County, which allowed it to be open as late as 3-4am in the morning. Down & Dirty was family owned and had the best BBQ in town. They also had rules. Rules that were followed or the husband and his boys would throw you out. Down & Dirty affiliated themselves with white customers and on some days the whites would frequent the bar side of Down & Dirty. I'd spent most of my day doing everything but job hunting and was on my way home when the owner of Down & Dirty asked me (after looking at my breast and telling me what he'd like to do to me), if I'd like to work there as a bartender. "You can drink all you want, keep all your tips and I'll pay you five dollars per hour," he said. It sounded like a good deal to me. I couldn't ask for anything better. Free beer and five dollars per hour. The tips were just crazy. When the owner found out my tips were doubling my pay he wanted to decrease my pay. Fortunately, I knew that I was the reason the bar was packed all day. No deal.

I didn't tell my mom where I was working right away. I didn't feel like hearing what she thought about it. Also, this was one of her hang-outs. I was there for a month before she found out I was working as a bartender. Once she found out, she commented, "I can't hang out at Down & Dirty because you're there." That was okay with me because I didn't want her watching and judging me.

Everything was going great. I was paying my bills and taking care of my baby girl. I had my eyes on a regular and noticed he was driving a red 5.0 mustang. He had gold in his mouth and fat pockets. He always had a conversation and only drank Heinekens. I liked this. When I finally got a day off, dude asked me if I wanted a drink. "No," I responded, "I can buy my own." I'll never forget, he gave me the strangest look, then walked off - only to return and ask me again. Again, I said no.

"Why not," he asked.

"For you to call me out my name when I don't want to talk to you later," I said. "No thanks."

"Hey," he said, "You're not like the rest of those chicken heads, now if I can't buy you a drink, what can I do for you?"

Mind you, I like money and I liked nice things. He had both. Plus, he was fine. Before the night was over I had a pocket full of money, a nose full of coke, a stomach full of wine and a man in my bed.

I awoke the next day with this naked man asleep behind me with his arm and leg across me, as though we were married. I slowly slid out of bed to go take a shower. I felt like crap and didn't really want to face him. I stayed in the bathroom so long that he finally knocked on the door and asked if I was all right. He then asked if he could shower and clean himself up. We went to breakfast and as I sat across from him, I kept avoiding his eyes. I learned that he was very blunt and open. The next thing out of his mouth was, "Hey, man I want you to know you didn't play out my pocket last night. You're not a whore. I like you and there's more where that came from." I relaxed and fell into a relationships that would soon turn into an all expense paid trip to Hell!

We went shopping the next day for new furniture. I guess he thought I didn't have enough. My stereo didn't sound clear enough, so a new one was purchased. After that I needed new clothes and shoes. My hair needed to be done by someone other than the project stylist. My daughter needed name-brand clothes. We needed jewelry. I needed gold in my mouth (that he would later try and knock out).

He slung dope while I tended bar, snorted powder and slammed shots. Saturday was my night to bartend and the place would get so crowded that I didn't have time to talk or let him rub on me while sitting at the bar. Saturday nights soon turned into World Wrestling Federation or what I called a free-for-all. There would be bottle-throwing, cursing, punching, biting, and me wildly slanging my blade.

We'd fight until the owner came and threw him out of the bar. I'd be left with a black eye or a busted lip - only to end up in bed with him kissing the lip he'd just busted.

This lasted a year. My mom had taken my baby girl so she wouldn't have to witness all the foolishness going on around me. Dude finally got arrested during a major drug bust in the area. I moved on to someone better (or did I?).

# CHAPTER 4

## *A New Birth*
## *(Not Spiritual)*

My work at the Down & Dirty was on and off. The owner would always come and bring me back after telling me about the crazy men I got involved with. He said I needed to take care of myself and my baby - I needed a real man. I needed to leave them fools alone. I took this as a proposition from him and ignored it.

For a while I kicked with this dude who was friends with my brother. I had his son living with me and my daughter until I found out that this fool was

on the down-low. I suspected it earlier on because
he'd always take long showers - sometimes bubble
baths (not the ones you'd prepare for your man after
a long day's work). On Tuesday nights he'd go into
the bathroom and stay for what seemed like forever.

I remember prying open the door one night. He
was chilling in my perfumed bath beads. I freaked
out. He explained that he was sore and just wanted
to relax. He said he didn't realize the bath beads
were scented until it was too late.

Soon, I noticed my nail polish would turn up
empty or missing. I remember lying in bed one
morning, before going to work, when he was coming
out of the bathroom. My brother had come to pick
him up so they could go south and 'handle some
business'. I don't know why, but I looked down at
his feet and noticed his toe nails were brightly
painted with my fuchsia nail polish. I lost it. I called
him all kinds of names, none of which his mother
had given him. My brother came in the room to see
what was going on. There I was, standing in the
middle of the bed screaming, "Get this faggot out of
my house." I explained to my brother about the
polish and until this day I can still hear my brother
say, while shaking his head in disgust, "Sounds to
me Hattie, like you've got yourself a situation." I
decided that he had to go.

I remember washing his clothes, so I could pack them for him, when I noticed a pair of underwear that caused me to sit on my laundry room floor - screaming and crying. The laundry didn't get finished. I grabbed all his stuff - tossed it in the dumpster out back. I couldn't believe I was dating a bi-sexual. I think I went on a smoke-crack-spree for three days straight.

My daughter was living with my mom. By this time she was 5 years old and in kindergarten. My baby was so cute and smart. I would pick her up and we'd stop at our community park. I would meet with my homegirls and their children and we'd make a day of it - drinking, smoking weed, laughing and just kickin' it. Each mother would take turns watching all the kids after she'd taken her hit of the joint. We'd then walk to the store, telling the children that 'they'd been good' and we were now going to get them some treats. Now that I look back on it - it was more about the mamas having the munchies and restocking our beer and cigs. We'd return to the park and to 'our' area.

At this time, the park was divided into four sections:

The gambling section

The runners' section (ran to cars to serve dope)

The dealers' section

And our section (which later became the geek squad - dope mixed with weed).

You're probably wondering when I had time to do all of this weed smoking and work. Well, this had become my job. Down & Dirty had a drug bust. I was accused of selling drugs out of his establishment (these were only rumors). There was friction between the owner and myself. He was determined to save his business; I was determined to save my butt. I either had to get used to being randomly searched by he police or quit. I quit. I began slanging weed in the park and out of my bedroom window. I had many customers but there was one that caught my attention. I'd make special bags for him and that led to more conversation, him selling for me, and me ending up with him. This was all good.

He was five years younger than me and he did whatever I asked. Not to mention, the sex was awesome. I found out during this period that I liked being carried. He loved to lift weights and I loved watching him do it. He loved to dance. So did I. We used to sit in circles and free-style. He loved weed and 'hangin out with the fellas,' as he would put it. That was great, too. It gave me time to hang out with the girls and get crumpled up. Then things changed.

I don't remember when or why but this dude started telling me that I needed to stop getting high - that he didn't want no junkie "B" for a girlfriend. Well, of course you know this led to a fight. I kicked him out, after which, the landlord stated that my house was under surveillance. I decided to go to Miami for the Goombay Festival and let my house cool down. While I was gone, my house was raided and my brother jailed. When I returned an eviction notice was nailed to my door. Now what?

I put my game level on high and got paid. I found a one-bedroom apartment. That's cool. My mom had my baby girl. She said she didn't want the police to take her granddaughter when they came for me (I guess you call that caring). I moved in and so did he. I got tired of fussing with him, so I chilled out on my going out and moved it all to my apartment. He couldn't say that I was in the streets anymore. Now the problem was, I had the hood rats hanging out at his crib. I couldn't believe he actually said, 'his crib' - which led to a fist fight and me kicking him out, again.

I decided I needed a job. I was drawing too much attention to myself from the police. So, I went to work. I started working as a maid, again. He calmed down, and moved back into the apartment.

A week or two goes by and guess what? - I'm pregnant:

This can't be so!

On my goodness!

I can't believe this.

I have to get rid of this!

I can't have another one!

Time to think!

Time to plot!

I won't tell him.

I'll get rid of it, quietly.

To those of you, reading this piece, I must let you in on something. There was a time in my life that I did acknowledge God as my Lord and Savior. There was this couple that I would go and visit once or twice a week for Bible study. But, in the midst of all my partying, men, drugs, and fist fights - I'd stepped away from all that I was taught. The couple, now deceased, were deeply rooted in their beliefs and being servants of God (True Servants).

Now, mind you, I'm a mess. A big mess. Trying to come up with a solution. I stepped to a friend who I knew was interested and told him what was happening. He was pissed. I didn't care. I just wanted his help. He promised to do it if I ever needed it. I knew strings were attached, but I'd deal with that later. "I'll leave the money somewhere for you to pick it up Wednesday," he said. "Don't tell me because I don't want any part of it." He didn't want to know if I did it or if I was just hustling him out of $350.00. I felt I was okay and could relax. I needed to get high and calm my nerves. It didn't matter because I wasn't keeping the baby anyway. I had to go over to the complex in which I used to live - to cop (purchase) my drug of choice (weed and crack). As I came back from the complex I noticed that Reverend Truth (that's what I called him) was working in his garden in the back of his house. I tried to walk by real quiet and fast. Not!

Without looking up he said, "I haven't seen you in bible study for sometime now. What happened?" "Nothing happened," I said. "I just stopped coming."

"How's everything going? How's your family and that little baby girl? She should be about 5 or 6, right?"

"Yes, sir."

I started to walk away, only to be called back. When I turned and went back he was just standing there rubbing his hands together. He took a long look at me. It was a look that I never liked receiving from him. It was the type of look that made you feel as though he saw right through you and knew if you were lying to him. I tried to avert my eyes - anywhere other than looking into his. He said, "You know what you're planning to do isn't going to happen."

"Reverend Truth, what do you mean?"

"How can I say this? Sister, you think you got yourself a little secret, but God sees and knows all."

"Yes, sir."

"I need to tell you that your plan isn't going to work. You see, you're pregnant and you don't plan on telling anybody about it. The father of that baby don't even know yet. You plan on getting rid of it, but your plan won't work."

Reverend Truth's wife came running out of the door and asked. "Brother, did you tell her what God said to tell her?"

They went on to tell me that I needed to change my life - that it was nothing good and that nothing good would come from it other than the blessing of my daughter (who wasn't born yet).

They laid hands on my head and stomach and prayed for me. I cried, told them I loved them, and walked away. I was arrested at 5:45am that Wednesday morning by N.S.B's finest and charged with aggravated assault. I was sentenced to the branch jail 'until further notice.' I was locked up, knocked up, and no one seemed to care.

I was told by my mother not to call home. She didn't want to have a phone bill she couldn't pay. She said I should have been doing the right thing and that she had my daughter and that was enough. My only contact was with my baby brother. He made sure I had money placed in my account while he was out. And when he was incarcerated himself, he still took care of me by turning money over from his account to mine. I knew from that point on that my brother was my one and only true family member.

I had a hard time in jail being pregnant. There were no luxuries. I still had that cold, hard bed with the one inch mattress, and the same bland food as the other inmates. There was also the shiny, polished-up stainless steel toilet that I shared openly with a roommate.

I started having heavy complications with the baby, so I was placed in a cell by myself and put on bed rest. My tray of food was brought up to me every meal and I refused everyone of them - which led to outside medical attention. This was the biggest mistake I made. Bigger than getting pregnant. I thought, "cool," I'd get to go out and see people. I couldn't wait to put on my street clothes and go to our clinic. I'd told one of my partners, "go up there so we can talk." I was ready to go, could hardly wait. To my surprise, the female guard came down and said, "I need to search you before we can leave." "What do you mean?" I responded. "Aren't I going to change my clothes?" She said, "No sweetie, you're going in this orange jumpsuit, and I have to handcuff you at your stomach and shackle your feet."

"Oh. Wow."

At that point tears, anger and shame visited me. I cried all the way to Daytona's Health Dept. I'll never forget the way all the employee's and patients were looking at me. I just held my head down in shame. I was examined with a guard outside the door. I couldn't wait to leave that place. I swore that if anything else happened, they'd never know. I'd rather lose the baby than go back out and be humiliated again.

Months had gone by when I met Dana from West Palm Beach. She was picked up for selling to support her drug habit. Dana was almost nine months pregnant and said whatever. I've never seen a 90 pound woman fight so much and so well. We became friends while we were there. I remember the night Dana went into labor. They placed handcuffs on her at the stomach, but did not shackle her feet because the baby could come. I also remember Dana coming back the very same night. The lights were out and I could hear Dana crying all night. The next morning I peeped into her cell. I asked her what happened. She told me, "They said the state will be here to pick up your baby if a family member isn't here by the time you're scheduled to leave. And they handed me this damn donut ring to sit on." I'll never forget the look on Dana's face and the size of that little donut ring. I, too, cried. I cried for Dana, for her baby, and for me and my unborn baby. This was the month of March. I started counting down how many days I had left before my due date arrived.

As the days passed I began to worry. I hadn't talked to anyone about coming to pick up and be responsible for my baby. I wasn't talking to the daddy. I actually hated him for doing this to me - not to mention the fact, he never came to visit, nor did he write.

Okay, I can do this. Maybe the baby will be better off in the care of the state. Could it be better in my care? No. I couldn't take care of myself. I remember another man of God coming to visit me and telling me what was happening in my life and that I would be given another chance. I believed Elder (I don't compromise) to be a true man of God from the time I was a little girl. I believed what he was telling me. He continued to tell me I just needed to change my way of living and thinking - I needed to believe in God and accept him as my Lord and Savior.

On April 12th, I was released. How? Why? I believe it was God and I thanked him. I had a daughter on April 14th. Notice, I thanked God. Yet, I didn't accept him personally as my Lord and Savior at the time.

The father of the child showed up, signed his name and we talked. And talked. He kept the apartment but it looked like he partied every night and slept all day. I cleaned the house (out of habit, not love), took care of his baby, and went to work. We started fighting again. I started using again. And with that came selling again. I found out he'd slept with all my partners. I didn't care. I'd made up my mind to sleep with 'Slick'.

I slept with Slick only after the baby's father confessed to sleeping around with the girl he later married. Slick was older, straight up, and he didn't judge me. He took care of my kids and he taught me a lot about the "game" from all aspects. He taught me where to get the money, how to get the money, and how to be by myself and be okay without having a crowd of leeches hanging on to me. I listened and learned. I even used some of the things he taught me on him. I knew Slick had other women, but I didn't see them. I was young and fine and received the most attention. I guess he felt he was training me. I enjoyed my days as well as my nights, which turned into mornings. I felt safe.

Time passed. I felt as though Slick had taught me more than enough and it was time to come up. I left Slick, only to run into Bubba.

# CHAPTER 5

## *Marriage*

Bubba. I remember the first time I said something to Bubba. He was walking down the street, pretending to be drunk. I noticed how he staggered across the street. It was hot this particular day. My girl, Black, and I were walking, laughing, and plotting. I remember her saying, "See, if I was crazy I'd approach that nigga right there. His pockets stay fat." (lights on!) I walked up to him and said, "Let me get $20 right quick and I'll give you $40 in five minutes or less." He laughed and asked, "What am I going to get out of this?" I told him, "An extra $20." He gave me the $20 and said, "You're sweet and all, don't make me kill you about $20." I told him if I was going to get him it would be for more than $20. I bought some weed and sold it for $40. I then bought a 20 and sold it too for $40. I found Bubba and paid him his $40. He refused it. He wouldn't take the $40, instead he gave me $100. From that point forward I started selling for Bubba. I never came up short. He began taking me out. We'd go over to Orlando, just for dinner. I would see something in the window while we were there and comment how pretty it was. The next day he was at my door with it, smiling from ear to ear.

Bubba was nothing like any of the others. Bubba had been places, seen things, and tried whatever was going on at that time. He was very articulate, highly educated, knew and loved expensive wine, liquor, and clothes. He knew how to finesse women of all nationalities. Most of all, Bubba knew how to please me like no other. If it took all night, Bubba went all night. If I wanted to be selfish, he allowed me to be selfish. If I wanted to be kinky, he allowed me to be kinky. If I wanted to be somewhat rough, he allowed that too. Bubba liked oils and creams. I found out that I too liked oils and creams. In this relationship it was always a surprise. We went on like that for two years, never repeating the same thing. Some days Bubba would come to New Symrna.Beach just to make crazy love and go back home. Oh! Did I forget to tell you Bubba was living with this chick in another city? They had four boys together and had been together for many years. While I'm at it, I may as well mention that he also used to pimp women.

It was time for Bubba to get a taste of his own medicine. He was 41 and I was 23. Bubba and I would often talk about having an open relationship. I think this was to justify the fact that I knew he had another woman on the side. I'd say, "Well, if you want to do that it's cool by me. But can you deal with it Bubba when you see me with someone else?" "I'm a man," he'd reply.

Two days later I was talking to this dude on the side of the road. We were talking about how crazy I was to be dating Bubba. He said he would have to leave me alone because he was too old to fight Bubba. I noticed Bubba standing in the middle of the street, but I kept talking to dude. The guy became a little uncomfortable and wanted to leave. I said, "Don't worry about Bubba. He has a woman. It isn't like that. We have an understanding." Old dude asked me if I really believed that. To be honest, I really did. It wasn't until I walked down to where Bubba was standing that I found out how open this relationship would be. Bubba grabbed me by my arm and started screaming in my face about disrespect! This nut had some nerve! I snatched my arm cut of his grip and started screaming back into his face, "Let go of my arm, Mr. Man. If you can't handle me talking to another man how do you think you're going to handle me in an open relationship. You're just mouth, Bubba. You want it all. You want to burn both ends from the middle, but you got the wrong one. Go home to your should-be wife and all those children." I walked off, not looking back.

At this point I was hustling, slanging coke, weed, and a little of me if I chose to. I saw a house I wanted and was determined to get it by Valentine's Day. That gave me a week to tighten up. I stopped smoking those two-quarter bags a day and only did my coke at the end of the day (5:00pm). My mom still had my first baby girl and sometimes the second one, too. She wasn't complaining too much by this time.

I went to the landlord of the home I wanted and she explained that there had been a fire in the kitchen and the walls were black with soot, but if I wanted I could get it. So I did. I scrubbed walls for days. I even had to scrub the wooden ceiling. I ripped up floors and replaced them with ceramic tiles. I applied polyurethane to the oak doors and placed carpet in each room. I tiled the bathroom and put in a new sink and toilet. I did some painting and paid someone to handle the yard work. I paid my friends and anybody I knew to help me.

By February 14th I was in my new place and feeling mighty nice. I had everything straight. It was time to party. Bubba heard about my crib. He stopped by and took over the party. He bought brand name liquor, stocked the bar and fridge with Heinikens. He bought a grill and threw steaks, ribs, shark, and shrimp on it. We had enough of everything. We couldn't run out, but if the liquor ran out he'd replace it. When the shrimp ran out he bought lobster tails out. I tried to ignore Bubba, but I couldn't. He hooked a girl up. I remember after the party was over I was cleaning up and Bubba walked over to me and asked, "Baby what are you doing? I'll pay someone to do that. I need to talk to you." I felt I needed Bubba as well. By now, you should know, this meant sex. Hot, mad, passionate sex. I thought for sure I was going to die right there. I remember lying in Bubba's arms that night and him telling me that he loved me and needed to be with me. I asked him, "What about the children?" I didn't care about the woman. He told me not to worry he was going to fix it. Friday night came. No Bubba. No call. Saturday around 2pm - still no Bubba, no call.

I called my girl, Black, "You need to come over and do something with me." Black was always

down with whatever. We walked over to Bubba's
partner and asked him to take us to Bubba's house.
This must have sounded crazy to him because he
laughed for about five minutes, took a swig of beer
and laughed some more. This response got me
heated. I said, "Are you going to take me or not?"
Bubba's partner knew about his other woman and
how she lived. I didn't. He said, "Hattie, I know
you're a bad bitch but I've seen this girl who hangs
with Bubba. I don't know if you should be going to
this woman's house." I told him that I didn't ask for
that piece of info as I got into his car.

All the way to Bubba's house he told me to stay
in the car and he'd go to the door and get Bubba. I
told him, "Do whatever." No sooner than we parked
the car in the front of the house and cut the engine
off, I hear cursing, glass breaking and a female's
voice screaming, "Get out! I don't need you!" I
looked at Black. She looked at me. I was like 'dang
- is it all that bad?' Black said, "Partner, are you sure
you're doing what's right? This could be his wife.
Bubba could be lying to you." I said, "Well, we're
here now and I'm going to find out." I went to the
front door and knocked. A voiced shouted, "What do
you want?"

"I want to know if I can talk to Bubba."

This high-yellow, tall, thinly built chick came to
the door with pink plastic rollers in her head (minus

one on the side) and a cigarette in her mouth. "Who did you say you were?" She was scanning me from head to toe. I said, "I'm Hattie from N.S.B. and I need to talk to Bubba." She politely turned and walked away. I could hear her telling Bubba, "Your whore from New Symnra Beach is here." She opened the door, invited us in, and apologized for the mess. She took us into the living room where Bubba was sitting. Black and I scanned the room, looking at the chaos. Furniture was turned over. Bubba's eye was swollen. He had scratches on his neck. She was bleeding. The baby was crying. I stood clueless in the midst of it all. I asked Bubba, "What are you doing? Are you fighting this chick?" She immediately went into a fit and started cursing. I noticed a very large butcher's knife in her hand. She said, "I'm going to kill both of y'all." She raised her hand and before I could do anything Bubba pushed me and Black out of the way. He pinned the chick's arm against the wall and was yelling for her to drop the knife.

The babies were screaming, so I grabbed them. She yelled, "Get your dirty hands off my children. You can have Bubba, but not my boys." She was screaming. Bubba was telling her to shut up and drop the knife before he let her go. She did. He let her go. As he began to walk away she pulled another knife from under her skirt and charged him. Bubba hit the chick so hard her rollers flew out of her head and she landed by the front door. I thought she was dead or seriously hurt. I started screaming and pounding on Bubba. "She's a female. She's a female. You can't be hitting her in front of those boys."

He walked outside with his suitcase, threw some C notes at her and said, "Hattie and Black, let's go." She came too, picked up her boys, snatched up the C notes and screamed, "You dirty so-and-so, I need more money." "I'll make sure you get it and I'll still pay my child support as before," he said. We got into the car as she screamed, "Hey, Hattie I can't wait until you start getting these same butt whoopings. Don't send the dirty so-and-so back to me!" We rode all the way home in silence, other than the sniffing sound as I pushed spoonful after spoonful of coke up my nose.

His partner dropped us off at my crib. Black and I went inside, got our drink on and got crumped up. Bubba and his partner had business to take care of. When Bubba came back he was in a really funky mood. I didn't like the vibes. He looked over at his suitcases and said, "Why are my clothes still in them suitcases?" I was looking crazy and said, "You haven't put them up yet, I guess." Right then, I should have placed him and his luggage outside that door. From that point forward it was a living hell.

I was taught to arrange underwear and how to properly iron and fold handkerchiefs. T-shirts went into a separate drawer. Ties were hung where only belts went. Shorts went here. Slacks went there. Button-down, pressed dress shirts face this way. Short sleeves were hung here. Jeans were starched, pressed, and put in their place. Canned goods were placed in order. Everything had a place. The floor had to be clean (how did he say it?), "Clean enough to eat off". I dusted every day. No dirty laundry was be left from one day to the next. His meals were to be served hot, not micro-waved.

I did this every day, without a word. This is what Bubba liked and I loved Bubba.. If this was pleasing Bubba, I was pleasing my man. When the weekend came, Bubba and I would go hang out. He'd set up the whole bar, not once but twice. I thought, "This is great." I was having a nice time. People were telling me how lucky I was to have Bubba as a man. I thought so, too. That would all change.

The day after all the partying, Bubba would count his money and start complaining about how expensive it was to keep a young whore like me happy. "Whore! You left your whore back at your old house." I waited to be attacked. Instead he'd laugh and say, "Yeah, I have a young one and I need to train her I see." I'd walk off. I wasn't trying to hear about this training he was going to be doing.

Bubba woke me up at 3:30 am one morning. He wanted breakfast. This was starting to get on my nerve and he knew it. Half the day was gone and Bubba wasn't back. I was worried - no calls, no nothing. At 8 pm Bubba came through the door. There was no fish and no fish smell. But I did smell alcohol. "What fish creek you've been on," I ask. "I haven't," and that's all he says. I was hot. 98 degrees hot.

When I got up the next morning, I didn't cook breakfast. I did cold cereal just because I knew he didn't eat cold cereal. As I poured the cereal, a ring rolled out into the bowl of cereal. "Oh my gosh!" I screamed for about 10 minutes.

I put it on my finger after counting 27 diamonds and a large one in the center. Oh my gosh! I ran into the bedroom and dove into the bed on top of Bubba, screaming and laughing with my ring smashed in his face. He just smiled and admitted that he thought I didn't want him. The ring had been in that cereal box since the night we went out together.

I said, "I do," a thousand times I think. I was going to get married. We were going to be married. I told my mother and she was okay with it. I told all my homegirls, my brother, and all his partners. We didn't do the church wedding. We went to city hall and were married. I took sister 'Vee' with me as a witness. Too bad she wasn't around to witness the rest. That night we paid one of my girls to babysit while we went to Orlando for 5 days. We left her with the house, filled the fridge, broke her off, kissed the 2nd baby girl (my mom kept the first) and dipped.

We checked into a suite and popped open the Don Perigon. I danced for my husband, feeling mighty nice. The second day we went shopping (no limit). I had so much stuff - he had to carry shoe boxes and bags, I couldn't fit anything else into the car. The third night I wanted to just relax and stay in. Not! He went out and hooked up with some old friends. I was in bed when Bubba came in with two dudes who were dressed like militant soldiers - they were talking about oppression. "Baby girl, get up. I want you to meet some alright friends of mine." I put on a dress and introduced myself. I sat for a few minutes then said, "It was nice meeting you two but I'm going into the bedroom and let y'all catch up." They said goodnight. Before I could shut the door all the way, I was flying across the room. When I landed on the floor I turned around and Bubba was punching me in the head. He held my mouth with his other hand as he whispered in my ear, "You ungrateful slut. How dare you walk out on my friends. I entertain your no good friends everyday of the week. Clean yourself up! Put on some make-up. We're going out and you better act like you're enjoying yourself." I did just that.

The next morning, I wanted to go home. Bubba (get this) wanted to make love. I refused and got the crap beat out of me. He threatened to throw me out of the window. Bubba got what Bubba wanted. I didn't talk to him for two days, unless he asked me a question. Flowers, a new dress and shoes, and another diamond ring came the next day. I cried. He cried. We made up.

Bubba didn't hit me for about a month. He decided, "You need to do something with yourself. You did graduate, right?" he asks. "Yes," I respond. "Well, you need a career. What do you like doing?"

I went to college to take a nursing assistant course. I graduated, received my certificate and found out I was pregnant. I didn't tell. (My secret) Friday night Down and Dirty had Chippendale male review. I didn't know if I'd go.

Bubba came home that day with a car load of my partners. He walked into the house and said, "These whores been looking for you." He pulled out a plate and dumped a pound of white powder on it. He even fixed drinks for them. I looked at my friends in disbelief, thinking, "Y'all acted as if you didn't hear him. Don't y'all  have a clue that he doesn't like y'all." I thought that if I told them openly how Bubba felt it wouldn't have mattered much anyway. Honestly, whose ears are open when they have a straw up their nose? I know I only heard what I wanted when I was getting crumped.

That night, I sat back with my wine cooler. No coke. Bubba came out and said, "Hey baby, it's male review tonight. Here's 100 one dollar bills. You got an outfit and shoes in the  car. I hope you like it." To me, Bubba had excellent taste in clothes and shoes. Neither was ever cheap. I went to the car and pulled out a black piece of material with a gold zipper that went from the back of my neck, between my legs, up to my chin. There was also a pair of patent leather pointed toe mules. The girls left to get dressed. I would meet them at the club. I showered, shaved and put the body hugging, booty-showing outfit on. I knew I looked good in it, but it was so revealing. I was worried he was going to trip. I asked him, "Bubba are you sure?" "Baby you look good. I'm not insecure. I'll pick you up when it's over." Bubba dropped me off and sat and watched while I crossed the street. All the men were watching, as well as the ladies. My partners were telling me how freaky my husband was. I told them I thought that the outfit was too short.

I only told Black that I was pregnant and that I
wanted Bubba and I to calm down. I was scared
either way we were going to get busted or he was
going to kill me. I had a nice time hanging out with
the girls, laughing and pointing at the men. But, I
would have rather been home, even if Bubba
was there.

That was the day that I learned 'you have to be
careful what you wish for.' A guy named Pop came
inside the club to tell me Bubba was outside waiting.
I said goodnight and left. Pop walked behind me
saying how he wished he was the zipper on my outfit
and how lucky Bubba was. He said he had been
trying to get with me since high school but I chose to
make him a brother figure. I laughed as Pop walked
out to hold the door open. Bubba screamed from
across the street, "Let that "B" get the door for
herself. That's my job to open the door for her, not
some broke nigger." I apologized to Pop and that
made Bubba crazy! He told me that he should have
made me walk home, I wasn't good enough to get in
his car. So, I started walking. He said, "Get in the
car now. Not in the front seat." I wasn't good
enough. "Get in the back seat." I did. I began saying,
"I don't want to fight. I don't want to fight," while at
the same time taking off my heels. We pulled up to
the house and I remember Tommy standing in my

front yard. I got out of the car and tried to beat Bubba in the house.

Tommy said, "Bubba I have $200, help me out." I heard Bubba say, "Hold on Tommy. Let me kick this "B's" butt and then I'll take care of you." By the time I got to the bedroom door, I'd been punched in the head. I turned to face Bubba and he kicked me right in the stomach. I scratched his face and spit on him. I remember Bubba taking off his belt and beating me with the buckle. I could stand the punches. I couldn't stand that buckle hitting me on my back, on my arms - it was like fire. So, I fell on the ground holding my stomach and buried my face in the floor. Bubba was screaming, "Fight me back. You usually fight me back." He took his foot and stomped my ribs and my face until I said, "Stop! You're killing the baby!" I remember hearing Bubba say, "Stop lying! Whores don't have babies." He walked out, left me on the floor.

I couldn't get up the next morning. Bubba came to the doorway and said, "Get up. Go take a shower." I couldn't get up. He helped me to my feet and put me in the shower. I didn't want him to touch me. He insisted and I let him. He dried me off, kissing me all the while. I tried not to scream out loud. I screamed on the inside. I screamed for loving Bubba. I screamed for hating Bubba. I screamed for marrying

Bubba. I screamed for the baby I would bring into this living HELL!

Bubba put me in the bed. He had to carry me because it hurt too bad to walk, sit or bend. Bubba was scared. "Baby, I'm taking you to a private doctor. Let me dress you." He did.

When we arrived at the doctor's building, I thought, "Is he coming in this place with me? I'm going to have him arrested." He must have been thinking the same thing because he dropped me off, gave me $1000, and said, "Call a cab."

The doctor examined me, said that I was pregnant and had three broken ribs. The doctor then walked me into a private room and said, "Mrs. Laws, you need some help. I know your husband did this. I can call someone to come and take you to a shelter."

I looked him in his eyes and said, "I'm fine. I don't need any help. Now, is my baby fine?"

"Yes," the doctor said, "but neither of you are safe."

I called a cab and went home. Bubba was there, waiting. When I came in he asked, "What did the doctor say?" I gave him the pregnancy results and the news about my ribs. I also mentioned what the doctor had said. Bubba commented on me not going back there and I told him that was fine, too. "I won't be needing a doctor, anyway," I said as I examined his expression. He was trying to figure out why wouldn't I need a doctor. I was pregnant. "Why won't you need a doctor?" he asked. "Because I'm not having this baby," I said. I went into the bedroom, shut the door, crawled into bed, and closed my eyes. Bubba burst into the room demanding answers as to why I didn't want his baby. "Do I look happy enough to carry a baby? I've lost so much weight," I said. I wore a size 5 soaking wet.

Bubba started crying. I told him that all we did was fight and the fights had gotten more violent. Instead of him kicking the baby out, I'd rather have a doctor take it out. Bubba walked out of the room and I cried myself to sleep - only to be awakened by a crazed man with a gun in his hand. He pointed the gun at my head. Looking at the gun and looking into Bubba's eyes, I felt dying would have been my better choice. I grabbed the hand which held the gun and told Bubba to kill me. I was a living zombie then and wouldn't have felt anything if he did shoot me. I may have even enjoyed it better.

Bubba left that night and I didn't care. I hated Bubba and everything about him. I talked to God that night. Five years had passed without me even acknowledging God, but that night I cried to him like I'd never done before. I remember waking with the Bible on Bubba's pillow. I walked through the house. He wasn't there.

Bubba returned after being gone a couple of days. He asked if I still felt the same. I did. We sat at the dining room table and he asked if we could fix the marriage. All I could do was cry. I no longer wanted to be with him. I no longer looked forward to hearing his voice. I no longer felt that he protected me from danger. I needed protection from him.

Bubba and I no longer got into bed at the same time. If I was awake when he came in, I pretended to be asleep. There's a law about saying no to your husband and he's supposed to respect that. Bubba didn't respect that law or me as his wife. That was it! I was done.

I told Bubba, "I need you to take me to the clinic (abortion). If you refuse, I'll get someone else to do it for me." He took me. I aborted the baby. I was actually glad. I wouldn't have to raise a baby, born into an abusive relationship. When I divorced him, there would be no tie that bound us.

I continued to pray in private for God to take Bubba out of my life. I remember having dreams of white people entering my home with lights on their heads and large dogs barking outside. I mentioned the dream to Bubba and he asked me to tell him about it in detail. He would try to figure out the meaning. I described cars, trucks, vans, and lots and lots of people I didn't recognize.

Bubba and I talked casually, never as husband and wife. We were more like roommates. I'd say good morning. He'd say good morning. Nothing more, unless one of us was leaving the house to run an errand. Nearly a month passed like this; then early one morning my dream came true. Four o'clock one morning, my house was surrounded by trucks, cars, vans, barking dogs, and strangers with lights on their heads. Bubba and I were arrested. My whole house was torn apart. Everything I'd worked for was gone. I had nothing. The one thing that wanted to stay (Bubba) was the one thing I most wanted, gone.

Our bond was $500,000 each. By morning, they'd dropped the figure to $250,000 each, plus collateral. The guys Bubba worked for bonded me out, instead of Bubba. They figured I'd at least pay some of their money back. I found out that Bubba had been coming up short. He told them I'd been robbing him. I couldn't believe it. I arrived home and the landlord was waiting. She told me I could stay, but not Bubba. I didn't feel good about the house anymore and told her I would be moving. As I cleaned out the house, I found all types of smoking utensils that I knew weren't mine. We didn't allow anyone to smoke crack or pot in the crib. It had to be Bubba's. I was disappointed about this, but too glad to be out of this mess to shed any tears for him. My thoughts were, "Run. Run. Don't look back." I was free.

Bubba wrote me. He said he'd give me a divorce if I wanted. He went as far as to apologize to me. I stopped reading the second page. I didn't need his apology. He had just taught me how to survive and how to hate men. I would be all right. That day, I told myself, "You're to never cry again, nor have any love in your heart for any man but your baby brother." And I did just that.

# CHAPTER 6

## *Divorce*

Divorce was something that I needed, but nothing that I wanted. I guess living with my grandmother and hearing her say, "No matter what happens, you're to stay with your husband, because in the end God would take care of it all," somehow affected me. For some reason, subconsciously I believed my grandmother, but as I looked back at my grandparent's life I can't seem to recall my grandmother getting the life (almost) stomped out of her. So, I decided I'd keep that where it was - in my subconscious mind.

The day arrived when I received my divorce papers. To be honest, I was sad. I felt that I hadn't done my part as a woman, nor as a wife. Not only had I disappointed Bubba, I'd also been a disappointment to myself.

I kept hearing this small voice say, "Until death do you part." I'd laugh and say, "Bubba was working on that."

Time passed and nothing was any better. I was cold, disconnected, not just with the world but with myself. It became easier to do things that I'd once said no to - not me. Now, it was just the opposite. I'd be the first to scream, "Here me," to whatever a person was fearful of trying or doing. I'd be the one to nominate myself. I had nothing to lose.

Remember: The dead has no spirit.

I couldn't feel any pain. I started selling more drugs. Anything that would bring me quick, fast money. I sold only to support my habit and my habit was out of control. That's not my opinion, it's what others would tell me.

I felt I was just getting started.

# CHAPTER 7

## *Anger*

There were men out there that I need to hurt, or destroy their marriages, whichever came first.

I began to make rules, as I continued to spiral out of control. Rule #1, the most important:

If he tells you how he feels, take all of his money. Don't hook up again. Ignore him.

I didn't have time to get emotionally caught up. Other rules were:

Never get too intimate.

He isn't allowed to kiss your mouth.

He isn't allowed to touch your breast.

If allowed, he's paid and nothing else comes with it.

Never allow your hands to stroke him.

Never assist him in positioning.

Never allow him more than 7 minutes, no matter how much he's giving. Seven minutes means seven minutes. After that the price starts again.

I was told that I had too many rules and that was okay. They were considered the tricks in my eyes, not me. They were paying for something I had and had to wear a condom. Really, who was being tricked? Men disgusted me.

I soon became caught up in sadomasochism. I wanted to beat, pinch, slap, bite, or spank the men I was with. Some even allowed anal sex to be done to them.

I decided to move to the opposite side of the tracks. I never realized how many white men were into having kinky sex and all kinds of sick things done to them. I got so caught up in bringing them pain, that I'd often find myself telling them to keep the money because  I enjoyed it so much. I'd see them again two or three days later.

This led to me tying them up - sometimes not releasing them even when they begged to be released. The more they begged, the better I felt.

I realized that being angry felt good to me. I was angry with everyone about everything. There were days I'd be angry because one of them would call me up and ask how I was that day, and if I was interested in partying with him. I knew this meant, "I want you to come and smack me around." I'd sometimes ask the married men, "Why don't you get your wife to do this?" They'd all respond, "She doesn't understand." Their response would anger me. Here was another dishonest S.O.B. He would have to pay. I would literally beat him until I got tired. By the time I was finished he'd be screaming, "Enough! Enough!"

I hated men. They always came up with an answer for cheating on their wives, never admitting that they were just disgusting and selfish.

One Monday night, Nick (is what I called him) called me over to party. Nick liked to look into a five foot tall mirror as I spanked him from behind. I thought Nick was really weird, but he was nice and he didn't ask me for sex. Nick wasn't like an ordinary man, to me. Nick liked his scrotum sack to be spanked. I always thought that was a man's sensitive spot. So, when he requested that I do it, I thought, "Dude's really into pain. I hope I don't have to hurt Nick. If he thinks he's going to reciprocate, I'm going to hurt him."

As I stood behind Nick, spanking him as hard as I could, he was screaming for more pain, I looked up and saw myself in the mirror. I saw a person whom I didn't recognize and I froze. It was at that moment that I saw the way Bubba looked when he was lashing out at me. I couldn't go any further with the spanking. I backed out of view of the mirror, changed my clothes, and called a cab. That day, I stopped looking in the mirror for any reason at all.

# C H A P T E R   8

## *The Comforter*
## *(not Christ Jesus)*

As time passed, I was having trouble trusting anyone. I felt everybody wanted something.

My children wanted time.

My parents wanted money.

My girlfriends wanted more free 'get high'.

And men wanted more sex.

I wanted to get away from that, so I had to change my game plan. I didn't say it was a better game, but it was definitely a different one.

The Game Plan:

No female friends were needed. Drop 'em all.

Take care of my children's needs.

Break mom off. She has the girls (I can't and won't take them with me).

No more spanking.

Find a male friend I can trust. Make sure he comes with benefits. (I do have desires).

I searched and searched, them Boom! I saw him at the store. He said, "Hey girl, what's up?" That was it. I knew he liked what he saw. So, I said, "Hey, I need to holler at you for a minute." We walked, talked and got caught up in conversation until we were in front of his crib. It was located in the right area - I had already noticed. I commented on it. He agreed. Red is his name. He was very intelligent, I mean extremely book smart. But I thought to myself, "I know I've seen this dude making runs and stacking paper." So, I told him that I had people that I knew who I didn't want to come over to the hood. I no longer wanted to hang out at their crib, either. It was now a get it and go situation. I found that I liked his set-up better.

Red allowed me to set up shop at his crib, if I promised to look out for him, when he wasn't catching any sales. No problem. It was the perfect set up or so I thought. Red had his set of white men that would drop by and spend a good bit of money. I figured Red couldn't supply them. Why should I miss out and let the money go - which led to minor problems. His customers would call and ask for me. This made Red hot! For a moment, I wasn't allowed to serve at Red's house. No problem. I met the customers down the street. Why not? It began to bother me so I would call them from a pay phone and handle my business from there.

Weeks passed and I hadn't talked to Red about anything. If I saw him I pretended I didn't - that way I didn't have to speak. I remember him calling out to me, "Black!" - that's what he called me. I didn't mind. Everything about me was black. My skin. My thoughts. My heart. How did he come up with such a perfect nickname for me? Go figure. I turned and asked, "What do you want?" He said, "There's a dude that said he sees you at the store and you won't say anything to him. I know it's you because he described you as having legs for days, blond hair and blue contacts." I explained to Red that I didn't want to hook up with that white man. Red asked if I would 'help him out.' He was in a bind. My first thought was to refuse. He did kick me to the curb, after all.

I asked Red what the white man had offered him. A hundred dollars to get me to speak to him. Uh huh.

I figured if Red got a hundred to do something as simple a task as that, I was going to get paid.

That night I pondered whether or not I really wanted to see that white man. He was probably just another freak that wanted a spanking, I thought. I would soon find out. I walked up the stairs to Red's place, stopped, and peeped in the window. I saw the white man. He was tall, with blond, shoulder length hair. He was standing, so I noticed he had quite a nice build - for a white man. I knocked on the door. I hadn't dressed in my best. In fact, I'd just pulled on a pair of cream colored tights, brown and cream double knit sweater over a cream turtle neck and a pair of Doc Marten boots. I thought I looked okay enough to say 'hello'.

When I entered the apartment, this blond hair, blue eyed, 6'3" man scanned me up and down, boldly. I was offended, so I said, "Take a picture. It'll last longer." I brushed past him and called Red in the room. I asked him if he'd gotten paid because 'whitey' had to go. I wanted to get high and he had to go. The white man was standing behind me as I said this about him. I looked at him and rolled my eyes. Red said, "Black, don't be so mean." I told Red I had to go. That's when Francis said, "I'll buy you what you want. How much do you need?" I scanned him, looking for wires or something to connect him to a cop or a snitch. He was offended. I told him to go home and he didn't move. He repeats himself, "I can buy you whatever you want." I laughed and said, "Pay me double whatever you paid Red." He said, "That's $200." "I know. I can add," I snap. "I'm black, not ignorant." He then adds, "And rude." "Whatever," I respond, "You don't know me. So keep your comments." He pulled out his wallet, turned his back and handed me $200. I sat down, pulled out a cigarette and he reached over to light it. I asked him what his angle was. He didn't answer. I asked if he wanted to get high. He said no. I went into the other room to get high.

I didn't smoke in front of others. There are probably four people that can say they've seen me smoke. One of them has died.

When I came out of the room, he was still sitting there. Just sitting there! I said, "You're not drinking. You're not smoking. Why are you hanging out here?" "So I can see you," he says. At that point I wasn't feeling him - he was creeping me out.

"Do you feel as if I owe you anything," I ask him.

"No," he says. "Do you shoot pool? Are you hungry?

"I'm getting high. Why would I want anything to eat? Where are you from? Are you real?"

He didn't answer. He just quietly repeated,

"Are you hungry? Do you want to shoot some pool or do you plan on staying in that back room getting high?"

"I'd planned on it but you're blowing my buzz."

"Good. So, we can go shoot pool, right?"

I told him that I didn't trust him and that if he switched out, I wouldn't have any cab fare. He laughed and looked at my shoes. He'd seen me take the money and place it in my sock. I laughed and said, "Well, it wasn't enough money to leave and go with you." He gave me another $100 and we walked out the door.

He held open the door for me. I wasn't impressed. This was how I got caught up with Bubba. We left and I didn't talk. I was scared. I'd never gotten into a vehicle with anyone I didn't know. Yet, here I was riding away - leaving my drugs and the safety of Red's apartment to go shoot pool - or be killed!

I must have had a look on my face, because Francis said, "I know you're not scared." "Should I be," I shot back. He said that I should have been more afraid at Red's than I was there with him. "I know Red," I said. "Exactly," he quipped, and left it at that. He took me to a pool hall on US 1. I walked in and some people greeted me. Others whispered their disapproval, loud enough for me to hear. I pretended I didn't. Francis asked if I was okay. Of course I was. I believed that no matter how much a white man talked down on you, he'd still go to bed with you - behind his wife's back and keep it a secret from his friends.

We shot three games of pool as I drank about six white Russians. Some of his friends stopped by. We talked. I checked everything out. There were just too many rednecks. I asked if 'getting it on with a black girl' was something he had fantasized about. I was sure, by now, he was a redneck as well. He laughed at my remarks and shook his head at the same time. "Hattie, I'm not the enemy," he said. "You'd like me if you gave it a chance and stopped being a hard butt. I just want to know you, no strings attached."

I was quite sure I'd heard that before. I knew it was the biggest of the biggest lies, ever. So, I said, "Sure, no strings attached." We finished our drinks. It was 2 a.m. and time to go home. I demanded that he take me home - take me to the place where he met me. He did and when we arrived he got out, opened my door and asked if he could take me to dinner the next day. I said sure.

"How much is it going to cost me?"

"I'm not sure, we'll have to wait and see."

"Here's my number."

"Thanks, I had a nice time. I know you did, too."

He got into his vehicle and left. I went inside Red's apartment. He had a new batch and told me to chill with him. I pulled out the money Francis gave me - not to spend, but to think about how I'd gotten it. I sat back and thought about how much of a nice time I actually had with Francis.

I awoke the next day feeling an emotion I hadn't felt for quite sometime - happiness. I can't explain why. I just knew I'd been doing something different that day than I'd done in two years. I was going to go out to dinner with no strings attached.

I showered, put on a body dress with a pair of thigh-high stockings and a pair of Doc Martens. Francis pulled up, scanned me and asked, "You're going to dinner with me right?"

"Yes," I answer.  "Is the way I'm dressed a problem for you?"  His face said yes but his mouth said no. I climbed in the car and we left. He rode around and around. I finally asked, "What's the problem?"  "I just don't know where to go with you dressed like that," he said.

"Home! Take me home."

"No."

We ended up at Red Lobster. I said, "Don't you

worry now, Master Francis, I promise to use a fork and a napkin." We sat down to order.

"Why do you do what you do?"

"What? Go out with white men that I don't know?"

Francis dropped me off that night, gave me $150, and explained that it was all the money he had on him.

"See ya later."

It was Monday when a dozen yellow stemmed roses showed up at my mom's house. I knew he'd sent them. He was the only one around to do such a thing.

I hadn't hung out at Red's for a couple of days. Francis was sending roses every other day, and calling on his lunch breaks. I was spending time with my daughters - enjoying them.

I decided I was going to get a job. The thought of it made me laugh. I got up in the middle of the night, while this craziness was going through my head, and put together a resume. I used skills I'd gained from having children, playing sports in school, and my last job as telephone switchboard operator in school. I was a people person by virtue of all the contact I'd had with people.

After completing the fairytale resume, I laughed. If I didn't get a job using it as a reference, it didn't matter. It was all made up anyway.

I did get a job, as a state certified nurse's aide. It felt great. I was going to do right by my daughters. It was time to take responsibility as a mother and give my mom a break. Good intentions are what I had. That's all they were.

I worked hard and soon found that I liked doing my job. I was caring - me, caring for another - not looking for anything in return. I loved listening to the stories of the elderly residents, no matter how many times they shared them. Those people weren't judging me. They needed me. My co-workers depended on me. That was a good feeling to me.

I still saw Francis on the weekend because of his job. I was cool with that. He asked me if he could make love to me after we'd been going out a couple of weeks and I laughed. "I wondered how long 'no strings attached' would last." He turned all red when I made that comment. "Would you rather I pay for it, like a trick?" he said. I punched him in the mouth, split his lip, jumped out of the van, and flicked him off.

I was pissed. What did I do? The norm. I went over to Red's house. Francis was there screaming,

"Why every time you get angry, you want to fight or get high?" I didn't want to talk. Thinking back, I don't even think I knew how to talk. I ran up the stair and slammed the door.

I went home after staying at Red's a while. I had to go to work but I didn't want to go high. I was afraid God would punish me for touching the elderly people while I was high. I really believed that He would allow something bad to happen to my daughters. That fear is what kept me from working while high through 17 years of drug abuse.

The end of the year was drawing near. I planned to file my taxes and rent a studio apartment next door to Red's apartment. Francis had a fit. He started asking if Red and I were having sex. Was that the reason I wouldn't have sex with him? That night we went out and shot a couple games of pool. I slammed about 12 lemon drops to hype myself up. Francis told me he wanted to make love to me. How could I do it, for free? I didn't love him. I knew that. What I didn't know is that I would soon feel something for him. What that something was, I didn't have a clue.

He took me to his large home, located a street from the river. He had a roommate he didn't care for and was contemplating a move.

What came next, I didn't see it coming. As we went into his place, Francis said, "Hattie, I don't want this to be a trick, either."

"Yeah, yeah, yeah."

"I don't want this to be a rush job."

"Okay, okay. Just stop talking."

I must admit, it was different. He was like a black man, trapped in a white man's body. I had no complaints. Francis woke me the next morning with breakfast. I showered and he took me home.

I moved into my apartment and moved out a week later. Francis went to the landlord and rented out the front duplex. He told the landlord that I planned on living with him. I became infuriated. I told Francis that I wasn't paying rent or bills and that I'd come and go as I pleased. He agreed. But every time I turned around, he was there.

Francis was very good at paying his bills. Every now and then he'd buy something for me. Then, he'd take it back. That didn't bother me. I'd usually tell him, "I didn't like it anyway." I also let him know that he was only there for financial reasons and when I wanted sex- the kind of sex he was always willing to give.

I'd often sit and look at how Francis would watch me. I d wake up and he'd be standing over me. No matter what I did to Francis, he stayed right there - telling me how much he loved me.

"One day you'll love me in return." That day never came.

Two years into that one-sided relationship, I was freaking pregnant! That was what Francis wanted. Before I had a chance to tell him, the curse comes - my monthly. I was jumping for joy. I told him, "No sex." I didn't care how hot I got when I was high. I partied every night until the sun came up. I quit my job. Francis wanted me to stay at home. He said he'd take care of me and my two daughters.

Four months passed and the smell of cigarettes began to bother me. One morning I got up to brush my teeth and puked all over myself. I sat on the floor because I was too weak to stand.

Francis came home that morning; he'd been vomiting as well. He thought he had the flu. I called a friend at the health department and she stopped by with a pregnancy test. "Hattie Laws, you're pregnant," she says. No way. I've had that womanly curse every month. Even if it stayed for two days or even half a day, it showed. That was enough for me. She told me to go to a woman doctor she recommended to be checked out. To my horror, after being checked out, I was five month's pregnant. Five @#%@# month's pregnant!

How was that possible? Why didn't it kick?

Why didn't it move? Why was this the first time I vomited? Was the other vomit associated with the white Russians and lemon drops? It's too late to abort!

I don't want this monster inside of me. Yes. Monster.

It had to be. I smoked every day, all day. I smoked blacks. I smoked crack and weed. I smoked cigs. And rinsed it all down with alcohol. I didn't want to give birth to it. How many toes and fingers would it have?

How many heads?

Would it have eyes, or a partial nose?

How come you didn't let me know?

Why didn't you allow it to move inside me?

Why the secret?

I talked to God, not expecting an answer. Five years passed without me talking to Him. Why should He answer me? Now, I'm afraid of the 'monster' inside me.

I figured maybe I could lose it. Maybe it was already dead. Yeah, that's why I didn't feel anything.

Francis was scared the Department of Children and Families was going to take me to jail. I continued to get high. No doctors. No check ups. No vitamins. No food. He then begin threatening to call Children and Families himself.

My mom found out. Thank you very much. Francis took me to Women's Clinic and came inside with me. They performed a sonogram. The baby was alive. But by now, I was completely dead. I didn't know what to do. I didn't have anyone I could talk to who wouldn't judge me. I felt bad. I mean really bad - about all the crazy decisions I'd made in my life. Nothing good ever came out of them.

I was placed on bed rest. I was five months pregnant, lying in bed thinking how awful a person I was. I didn't even look at the monitor when the nurse tried to show me the baby. I guess I couldn't look at it. I didn't want to see the damage I'd done. I was sick. I was so sick.

I was told that if I didn't keep the crackers and water (my only means of food) they'd feed me intravenously. So, I ate toast with peanut butter, and forced myself to drink milk. I gained a whole 15 pounds my last four months of pregnancy. I felt good about the weight. Yet, I still couldn't accept knowing that I'd abused this 'thing' growing inside me.

It started moving on a regular basis. I thought to myself, "Maybe he was too weak to move before." That thought would send me into a crying fit. Then,

I'd think about my two daughters and that would make it even worse. I would become depressed and didn't want to eat. Francis would bring home strawberry ice cream. I like that. What I didn't like was the way Francis looked at me whenever he entered a room. Not once did he ever ask me if I was okay. Never asked me what my plans were. Never came inside the doctor's office with me. Never asked me what the doctor said. He'd just stand back and watch from a distance. He slept in another room. When I got up in the morning, he would be gone. I wondered sometimes if he was coming back.

One day I passed his room door. He'd placed a mirror on it. I stood still, looking at how I must have looked at him. Remember, I'd stopped looking into mirrors awhile back. Now, there I was. Standing right in front of a full length mirror. I looked like a poster  child for Feed the Children. It was the scariest, ugliest vision of me that I'd ever seen.  I wanted to move. I couldn't stop looking at myself. I no longer looked anything like Hattie. The healthy, smiling, go-getter. Where was she? Why had she left me? I wanted her back? Was I supposed to die like that? Why are you doing this to me?  I held my stomach as I asked that question. My other two didn't do this to me. Why you?

I didn't know. But I decided that I was going to do what I needed to do. I was an addict, pregnant with a baby. Yes. A baby. The baby didn't ask to be placed into this situation. "You know what," I said, "I'm going to take care of you. I don't want to have a retarded baby, even if I don't plan on keeping it."

Francis came home that day and found me in the living room reading a book, at that time I was into Dean Koontz and Anne Rice. I'd cleaned the house, washed up and pinned my hair, and put on a dress that didn't fit me. I must admit, I felt somewhat better. I did this same routine for about ten days, until my water broke.

Five o' clock in the morning. It was crazy! I went to tell Francis that I needed to go to the hospital because my water had broken. He looked at me and said, "I need to shower for work. Can you call your mom to take you?" I looked at the man standing in front of me. With anger and disgust I said, "You coward! The baby's coming." I began slapping him and pulling his hair. I picked up a bowl from the dining room table, to break on his head, but he ducked out of the way.

I called my mom and she clicked. "Tell that so-and-so to take you. I'm not dressed yet!" I got into his car and he jumped in. My baby girl got in and I buckled her up. The pain was killing me. Francis was screaming. My daughter was asking if she could have a baby brother. I was telling her yes. Francis' voice was starting to get on my nerves.

I knew what his problem was, he was afraid that the cops were going to be called to the hospital. He was going on and on. I couldn't take it anymore. I reached over and grabbed a ballpoint pen and stabbed him in the shoulder with it. He screamed. I screamed. I grabbed the steering wheel, a car was heading straight towards us. He grabbed the wheel but I wouldn't let go. We crashed into a chainlink fence, an inch from a telegraph pole. Firemen ran outside, pulled my daughter from the back seat, and then pulled Francis out. He was bleeding. Somehow he pulled the pen out of his shoulder.

The people in the other car were my mom and oldest daughter. Talk about being blessed.

By this point all I wanted to do was take my children and die. I wanted to protect them from the things I'd been a part of. I thought about how many times in earlier years, I'd heard, "If parents did drugs, it was likely that the children would too." It was a scary thought, picturing my babies strung out, living like whores, hating everything and everybody. It was a cycle I wanted broken. I was scared.

When and how were my next questions. When does it end? How does it end? If history really does repeat itself.

I rode to the hospital in my mom's car. She had to go to work, but stayed until I gave birth. The baby tried to come out feet first. He flipped around and the cord became caught around his neck, they had to remove it.

"Lord, please don't let him die. I'm sorry for what I've done. It wasn't his fault. It's me. I'm the one you're mad at. I'm the junkie, not him. Please let him be all right. I promise I won't use again. Just let him live. I know I don't talk to you daily. I don't even acknowledge you unless I'm in trouble. I'm too nasty. I'm a junkie. You don't talk to these kind of people. That's why I stopped talking to you. I was ashamed and didn't want you to see the kind of person I was. I didn't want you to see what I had become, but you don't have to look at me. Just save the baby. He's innocent. I promise, I won't mess with you about anything else. You don't have to save me. You can let me die."

The doctors asked me to turn on my side and hold still. They made me have a contraction, removed the cord, and turned him around, all at one time. They pulled him out. He was alive. It was a boy. A boy. He was so little. I wanted to touch him.

He wasn't crying. Why wasn't he crying? "Lord, why isn't he crying? Oh, please. Oh, please. Let him cry! Let him cry! I do want him! Jesus, I do want him!"

He started crying. I told the Lord thank you quietly and began to cry myself.

# CHAPTER 9

## *Going Through*

"The baby won't eat," said the nurse. "I need you to try feeding him. He's hungry but he won't swallow. If he doesn't eat, we'll feed him through his veins." He was so tiny and pink, with a head full of hair. He was looking right at me as I tried to get him to take his bottle. Something was wrong. I fed him for an hour straight and all that was missing from the bottle was two-ounces. I started crying. He started crying.

I started talking to God, again. "I know I promised I wouldn't come to you for anything, but the baby won't eat. I need you to fix it. Please. I need

you to fix it." The nurse came in and took him out of
the room to be changed. "He's crying and won't
stop," says the nurse. "We're going to bring him in
the room with you so he doesn't disturb the other
babies." I got out of bed and walked over to the
square glass box they had him lying in. I bent over to
touch him. He was so little. I picked up his hands
and counted his fingers. There were ten. I lifted his
legs. They were so thin and pink. I checked to see
how many ears he had. I looked for something. He
started screaming. I stood and stared. I thought, "Oh,
no. He's crying like this because he's a crack baby.
Oh, no. I'm not going to be able to take this." I
started crying. Crying because it wasn't his
fault. I was frustrated. He wouldn't stop that
aggravating crying.

"Lord, I need him to stop." I walked away and
cried. The nurse came in and said, "Aren't you going
to stop him from crying?" I looked at her and said, "I
tried. He won't stop. Can you take him back?" She
took him back into the nursery. I felt as though I was
abandoning another child. So, I told her to bring him
back. I asked her how long we were able to stay
there. She left and brought a doctor who told me that
they were waiting for Department of Children and
Families. I asked why. I knew I wasn't dirty. I was
told that because of the way I cared for myself and

the baby during the pregnancy, there were some concerns. The second day, my mom came to pick us up but she wasn't allowed. The baby was being tested for drugs and being monitored. He was losing weight. The doctor told me that A.J. (the baby) was a S.I.D.S. kid and they were giving him three days to live. If he made it three days, he would live a week, at most.

They brought him in to see if I could get twenty ounces in him before they had to put feeding tubes in him. I placed him in the crib and cried as he cried. It was at that moment that I began to pray. Once again, there I was praying to the Lord, hoping he would hear me. "Lord, this is the second day I've been here with A.J. Can you tell me Lord, why did you allow me to have him only to let him die? I know I didn't want him but I've changed my mind. Now, I don't know what to do for him. He's losing weight. He won't eat. Please! I know You know what the problem is. Can you let the doctor see the problem?"

As I prayed this prayer, a dark skinned man peeped his head into the room. He didn't have on a white lab coat. He didn't have a stethoscope. He walked over to the crib and said, "Is he your son?" "Yes," I said. "He's beautiful. Ma'am, I want you to know that your baby has a birth defect called cleft palate." I must have looked crazy because he went on to explain what it was and how one gets it. He asked if the father had been born with one. I didn't know. He said, "I can't check your baby because I'm only here from Gainesville to check on my patients. I'm a surgeon who repairs cleft palates. Your baby can't eat with a regular bottle. I've got some in my car, I can give you two to use for now."

He showed me how to hold the baby during feeding and how to sleep with him. He gave me his card and said, "I'll point this out to the pediatrician." I cried and cried. I thanked the Lord for sending me an angel.

That night a feeling came over me, letting me know that it was God that sent the dark skinned man to us. How else would he have found us? He sent the bottles up. A.J. finished up the 4 oz. bottle with no problem. I was so happy. For a minute, anyway.

It dawned on me that Francis hadn't been to the hospital, at all! So, I called the house. He answered the phone and I could hear music and voices. I asked, "Why haven't you been to see the baby?" He said very bluntly, "I'm afraid." I flew off the handle. I wanted to kill him! I wanted him out of the house. "I'll be home tomorrow and I don't want you there or I'll burn it down." He wanted to know if it was a girl or boy. I wouldn't tell him. I just hung up the phone.

I reached over and picked up A.J.'s little body. Holding him out in front of me, I told him I was sorry for hurting him. I really meant it. "I want you to know I love you and I promise to take care of you. I'll never abandon you." He was looking right at me. I know what it feels like to be abandoned, trust me. I'd been in that situation times before. "You need me and I need you. I guess we need each other. By the way, you have two sisters I'd like for you to meet and they need me too. I guess everybody really does need somebody. Sometimes anybody will do, as long as they don't leave you."

Here I was, talking to my baby boy about being neglected and abandoned. Something I myself had done over and over to my very own children. I needed and wanted help - at that moment, anyway.

Francis came the next day to pick us up. He wanted to look at A.J. I refused that request without a second thought. I told him that he didn't want to see him earlier so I figured he didn't really want to see him right then, either. We rode all the way home in silence. Francis tried to bring the baby and his carrier into the house. I wouldn't let him. I told him to carry the other bags in. I remember how he just stood and looked at me. I stopped in my tracks and said in a cold voice, "How long do you plan on staying here?" He called me an evil, cold black woman. I took it as a compliment and said, "Thank you." I placed the baby where I could keep my eyes on him and at the same time make sure Francis couldn't or wouldn't touch him.

At night, when A.J. cried, Francis would try to check on him. I'd tell him not to go near "my baby". Even though I was tired, I still refusde to accept any help from Francis. I didn't want his help. What I really wanted him to do was leave and never come back.

A.J. was a lot of work. When feeding him, he had to be held at an 80 degree angle, at all times. He was allowed two ounces and needed to be burped in between them. He needed to be at an 80 degree angle even when he slept. If I laid him down, a wedge was to be placed behind his back to keep him on his side. His head had to be raised to allow him proper breathing. And when he cried, there was no sound. Every now and then, the monitor light would flash and I'd go running. I'd find him all red and sweaty from where he'd been crying. That scared me. So, I moved Francis into the baby's room and A.J. into the bedroom.

We walked around like zombies. Not talking. Not speaking. We only asked each other if either had a light for a smoke. When the children came, he took them to the beach or pool - wherever they wanted. They stayed gone 'til dark. That was fine with me. I needed to think about where I was headed, with three children, no job and no place to call home.

I could hear talking coming from outside. I heard a voice that I wasn't used to but one I had heard somewhere before. I got up and went to the door. There was Francis with his mother. She was standing at my door. This little, 5', white headed, frail-bodied, elderly lady looked up at me and said, "I've come to see the baby. I need to see if he's my son's baby."

Now, let me tell you about this little lady. She always spoke her mind and would let you know it. When I first met her, she looked at me and mumbled under breath something about Francis liking black women just as his father had, that we weren't any good and that he should have had fun with me and nothing more. I told her to go visit Satan and walked out of her house. She would call the house to speak to her son, but if I answered she'd hang up.

I remember when she fell down and needed someone to care for her. I had no problem doing it. She couldn't talk - but she'd lay there, staring at me with those cold, blue eyes. The doctor told Francis that she wouldn't make it. I felt bad. I started praying for this lady to live. Is this funny or what? A sinner

like me, praying that God would spare this lady and
not take her right then. Come on!

I thought about it later. "Lord, don't I have a lot
of nerve praying for someone else." I even took my
hands and rubbed her body up and down as I prayed
for her. Well, I can say this, she lived a whole year
and some months.

She walked into my house without speaking and
walked into the room where my baby was. She
looked around like she was at the city dump. She
even commented on the furniture. She walked over
and cleaned her hands on her hanky, handed her
purse to Francis and picked up A.J. She inspected
him as if she was about to purchase a fine piece of
crystal. She looked over at me and said, "If he didn't
look so much like his father and his grandfather, I'd
say he was just another 'nigger' baby." Francis
screamed, "Mother," as I tried to grab this little, old
lady. Francis shoved her bag into her arms and told
her to get out of his house. He put her in the car and
drove her home. I couldn't believe that this was the
same woman I'd prayed for.

The next day she called and told me she had
nothing against me and my baby. It was just that in
Germany, where she was born and raised, she was
taught that you stay with your own kind - that all I
was doing was causing problems for my son later on

in life. He would never be accepted as a white person, nor as a black person. I hung up the phone.

I later received a solid oak, old-fashioned crib, delivered to the house. She gave Francis an envelope with $1000 to buy the baby clothes. I refused the crib. And the money. A month later, she was dead. Did I feel bad? No. I felt bad that Francis no longer had a mother. That night I moved out and moved into my mother's place. I told Francis that I no longer hated him. I apologized for hurting him and allowed him to hold A.J., his son. I even suggested that he come and visit. I just didn't want anything to do with him. I wanted to try and live a different kind of life style. . . .clean and sober.

# Chapter 10

## *Backsliding*

There I was, at my mother's with all three children. I was there three weeks, tops; I couldn't take it anymore. Between my parents and their screaming arguments, my mother screaming at me about what the children weren't doing one minute and cursing about what they were doing all in the same breath - I needed to get away. I needed to think. I often thought about deaths; to me it always seemed better than the life I was living.

I needed to be around people who understood my problems, people who knew what I was going through or could relate to situations at hand. I paid my dad to watch my son. He was about three months old. My oldest was ten and the second girl was five years old.

I remember leaving the house some days and thinking, "I'm never going back." I don't think it would have mattered to them. They seemed to get along with each other without me there. So, I stayed gone for two or three days at a time. I'd call and my mother would tell me that my children missed me and I needed to come check on them. I would come, clean the house, shower, and watch t.v. - I knew I needed to be there with them. I had no problem with that. I did have a problem with my mother telling me how to talk to them, how to chastise them and what to cook for them. I knew how to do those things. I just wasn't there to do them. Don't get it twisted. I tried to be there. But, I found out that with drug addictions, not only do we make excuses, we look for excuses.

When my mother complained, I took it as an excuse to leave. She didn't want me there, anyway. That allowed me to leave without having a guilty conscience. If my step-dad complained about not having any pocket change for himself, I would tell my mother, "I'm going to go and make some money." That would allow me to leave. It got to the point that any excuse would do.

The house was too hot. Certain relatives were visiting, that I didn't like. It got so bad I didn't want to be around my family at all. I didn't want my children to see me. I weighed 110 pounds at that time.

I went home one day out of the week, did the girls' hair, ironed school clothes for a whole week. I sat down with them and did their homework for the entire week. I bought groceries for that month, gave my mother a child support check, kissed my children and left, all in that one day.

As I look back, I did that up until my oldest daughter was in the 11th grade. The second child was in the 6th grade and my son was in kindergarten. I realized that my life was completely out of control. I even made arrangements for my oldest to know where I was on Friday nights. She knew I was on drugs. I would tell her to come to a certain house at a certain time and I would go down stairs and give her money to go out with her friends. She never asked when I was coming home. She'd only ask, "Mom, are you okay?" I'd say yes. When I told her I loved her, she wouldn't say she loved me back. I understood and accepted it for what it was - the truth. Why would she love someone like me?

Knowing this only sent me into a deeper, darker part on the inside. I never knew a body had so many depths of darkness.

I continued living my life as if I had no reason to live. It got to the point where I would call my oldest daughter and have her iron the younger children's clothes, do their hair and pick them up from school. It got to where she and my mother were there for the middle girl's homework. My mother would meet me at the big house or Publix to get money. Why? If I went to the house I'd have to hear her say, "Girl, these children need you and you need to take care of your responsibilities. I can't keep watching these children. I'm tired!"

Tired? Tired? That was an understatement. I was so tired! I was sick and tired of being sick and tired. There were days I'd awaken only to lie in bed and wonder, "Lord, why waste your time waking me? I'm not going to do one thing today to make you proud of me. Lord, if I were you I would have been given up on me."

# Chapter 11

## *Pride, Before Destruction*

Yet, here I was, another day.

This was starting to make me angry. I was tired of living like that. Smoking crack. Snorting powder. Puffing weed. Slamming shots. Tricking. Every day I was tired of doing this and that. I couldn't stop on my own!

"Lord, would you please not wake me up tomorrow, if you truly love me?"

As time went on I was walking through the day without acknowledging my surroundings. Half listening. I'd often find myself talking to myself about finding a better way. "There has to be something better than this. Because something as bad as this can't be living. I'm just taking up space. Let someone else fill it up. Someone that will make you happy, even proud."

And yet, grabbing for hope, I tell myself I don't have to live like this. If other people could live clean and sober, I knew I could live clean and sober. I went home.

I cleaned up, washed my hair, did laundry and walked my daughter to school. I remember her asking, "Are you going to iron and wash all my clothes?" Baby girl was now in the 5th grade. I told her no. She then asked if I would come pick her up from school. "Yes. I'll pick you up." She then gave me a hug. It was a good feeling. I missed my baby girl.

I thought back to when she was two years old, following me around foot-to-foot. There she was that day trying to talk like a big girl. I went home and cooked dinner. I felt so good. I even baked homemade cookies. I did that for seven full days. I was happy and at the same time, scared. My biggest fear was I knew it wouldn't last. No matter how good I felt about myself. I knew deep down inside it just wouldn't last. I say that because at the point when you're trying to do your best at staying clean, someone comes and freely offers you drugs.

It could be right after saying, "I did this for seven days. I can do this!" It doesn't matter how much you resist. It doesn't matter how you, yourself know this thing (addiction) is destroying you and everyone in its path. You'll look down and in the very palm of your hand you'll notice that you are now holding a piece of crack.

I would lie and say, "I'll just put it up for one of those bad days." Keeping it real, people - Every day of my life that I used, was a bad day for me. Some days were worse than others. I would just tell myself over and over that I wasn't as bad as the others. That way it made it a little easier for me to use.

Even when my mind would tell me, "You don't have to live like you're living." I'd say to myself, "Well at least I'm not stealing or hurting anyone, but myself." When moments like that would come, I'd often feel guilty about everything. I'd even go back as far as when I was 17. There I was, an adult, thirty years old - looking as far back as the age of 13 and trying to find a point in my life when and where I went wrong. I never was able to pinpoint a time.

My thoughts were all in a jumble and nothing made any sense. I tried to find the problem. My solution was suicide. It seemed to be my only answer for, oh, so many problems.

HATTIE LAWS

I left the house and went over to Red's. I remember that day because I wasn't my usual, talkative self. Red kept asking, "Are you okay?" "Yes,' I said. "Well, why are you sitting over in that corner where I can't see you?" (I didn't want to be seen). I divided up my package so Red could do whatever, however. I just wanted him to stop asking all those questions. It didn't work. I could still hear him talking; I wasn't answering. I even heard him say, "Man, I don't know what's bothering you today, but I'm going to talk. You don't have to." I heard a knock at the door. It was Shay. She stopped by to say hello.

She had her own. She offered. I told her no thanks. "I have my own." Shay was looking confused. I was sitting where she'd normally sit and she didn't know where to sit. Red said, "Shay, come sit over here. Black is tripping today. I've been talking to her and she hasn't said two words." Shay asked, "Baby girl, are you all right? That doesn't sound like you."

"I'm straight. You two have each other now. So, don't worry about me."

I was then smoking back to back, nonstop. That day I wasn't drinking pink lemonade. I was drinking shots of liquor. I could hear what sounded like my heartbeat drumming in my ears. I took my hand and placed it on my heart. It was beating way too fast.

My hands were shaking to the point where I couldn't hold the glass. I could hear Red and Shay's voice in the background but couldn't make out what they were saying. I heard a third voice. It was so soft. Like a whisper. It was calling my name. It was calling my name. Or was it? "Maybe I'm tripping."

It then says, "Put the glass down. Put it down, now." I got up and staggered into the bathroom and I locked the door. Red and Shay came to the door. I tried to look into the mirror but I couldn't see. I felt bad. I turned to the door and started puking uncontrollably. I was crying and puking. They were calling me. "I'm okay," I told them. I sat on the bathroom floor for a while and continued to cry. I stood to wash my face and mouth out. I looked into the mirror and the word 'coward' came from my lips. I cleaned up my mess, apologized to them, and left.

Two days passed without me talking to Red. He called wanting to know what was up. Shay came by and I just peeped out the window at her. Never answered her knock. I didn't want to talk. I was thinking of another way to die. A way that wouldn't take long. No suffering.

"I got it." I got dressed up, applied makeup, put in my contacts and did my hair. I walked down the street and people commented on how nice I looked. "Are you kidding me?" I must have been an actress because on the inside I was black as coal. And dead. I felt nothing. I saw nothing but darkness. I no longer saw pretty colors. Everything I saw was always black.

There was nothing but the sound of me screaming as loud as I could scream. No one heard me. "I must be walking around in a sound-proof box." People were all around saw me but no one really listened. "I give up. No one knows my pain." They only saw me - an addict. Hopeless. Worthless. Lost cause. I too, saw the same thing everyone else saw. I didn't like it. I apologized to my babies . I apologized to my mother for being a failure to my children. I apologize to my brothers for not being a big sister to them. I apologized to God for what I'm about to do (or so I thought).

I was walking, oblivious to my surroundings. I stopped and realized that I was at the top of the Martin Luther King, Jr. overpass. It was located above railroad tracks. You'd be surprised how many people pass you by and never take notice of what you're doing. I was standing in the center of the overhead. Traffic was coming and going nonstop. I was crying. Leaning over the top of this bridge. I measured the distance from the top to the ground.

The way life was going, I'd jump and probably wouldn't die. I'd probably be paralyzed and that would be even worse. I'd then be a handicapped junkie. No thanks. I would wait for the train.

I stood there crying for what seemed like forever. A train whistle finally sounded. It was moving slowly. I needed it to pick up speed. It started to move at a pretty good speed. "Don't worry. If you time it just right, you won't feel a thing."

I leaned. I waited. Cars passed and blew their horns. I continued to lean. The train stopped and went into reverse. I screamed. "I don't believe this. Why would you do this? I don't want to live anymore, God! Why don't you go ahead and let me die?"

I sat at the bottom of the bridge and cried hysterically. A vehicle pulled up. A man said, "Are you okay?" It was my nephew. He helped me into his S.U.V. and took me home. I remember him telling me, "It always gets worse before it gets better. But, it does get better."

# CHAPTER 12

## *This Is Death*

I had a dream that night. I dreamed I was dead.

I lay in a pearl white coffin, dressed in white with white gloves. I could see everybody's face. I could see my mother's face. She was crying. I could see my children's faces, my brothers' faces, as well as my grandmothers and aunts. They were all crying because I was gone! That caused me to cry.

It was strange because it seemed as though I was there (an out of body experience). I could hear their conversations as I walked around. I realized that my family didn't hate me. They actually wanted to help me without pushing me away at the same time. It was at that moment that I died. All the hate and confusion and denial died inside. I wanted to tell them I needed help and that I loved them too. That I was sorry for all the hurt I'd caused them.

I awakened to hear myself saying, "I'm sorry," over and over again. "I'm sorry. I'm sorry." My face was covered with tears. I looked around and found myself in bed. Everyone else was still asleep.

"I need some help. I really do." Not just any help. I needed honest to goodness, sincere help! I went outside and sat on the porch. The door opened up behind me. It was my baby girl. I was watching the rain. I saw the moon behind the trees every time the sky lit up. I looked over at her - watching me. I could see she'd been crying. "Are you okay," I ask. She gave me a great big bear hug and started crying again. "Girl, what's wrong with you?" She told me she had a bad dream. "What about?" She looked at me and said, "You! You were dead! You were lying in a white coffin, dressed in white with white gloves on your hands. Mommy, I'm scared! Please, don't leave tonight. Please, stay home. Something bad is going to happen to you."

I told her to stop crying. "It was only a dream. Go back to bed," I told her. "Promise you won't leave," she said. "I promise."

Now, I was scared. How can two people have the same dream of death at the exact same time? Maybe, just maybe, my time had come. I cried and began talking to the Lord with my arms stretched out wide. Palms up. I cried out, "I surrender! I surrender my heart, soul, and mind. I surrender every thought, every problem, every pain, every heartache, every lie, every broken promise, every failure, and all my children. I surrender to you, Lord! I can't do this on my own!"

It was at that true moment that I did die. I died so that I could live.

# CHAPTER 13

## *Resurrection*

There was feeling. It was all over me. I couldn't move. All I could say was, "I'm sorry. Forgive me. I'm sorry. Please, forgive me and all my wrong doings. Forgive me of all my nasty ways. Forgive me of my sins!"

I was bent over and there was a pain on the inside that I couldn't explain. The pain hurt so bad, yet in some strange way I felt better. I stepped out into the rain and washed my face.

I needed to talk to someone that could help me. So, I walked three or four blocks toward a minister's house. I knocked and I knocked. No answer. I needed somebody to help me. I walked toward Howard Street and Mary Avenue to a house on the corner. I stared. And stared. Never once getting the courage to ring the doorbell. I left.

I needed help. I needed someone real that wouldn't judge me, right then. I walked in the rain. My clothes were soaked. I saw head lights coming my way. I walked faster. "These people might think I'm high and tripping. I'm not and I don't want to explain myself, right now."

I can't explain the feeling I had. I wanted to shout for joy. I wanted to dance. I wanted to clap my hands. I felt excited. Excited about being excited.

The car pulled up. It was Debbie. She said, "Get in the car. I'll take you where you're going. What are you doing in the rain?" I answered, "I'm looking for someone." She said, "Well, maybe I can help you find them." I told her, "I don't think so. I'm looking for someone who can help me."

I told her to take me home. I had a carton of cigs and I wanted to give them to her. I told her that I didn't smoke anymore. Debbie was looking at me like I'd lost my mind. She had just seen me the day before, getting high and smoking cigs. She smiled and told me to stop playing with her.

We got to the house and I gave her half of the carton. I gave the other half to my step-dad. He was looking crazier than Debbie. I smiled and said, "I'm not going crazy." I felt good. I knew where I need to go.

"Can you take me to Sheldon Street? There's someone I need to see," I asked Debbie. "I thought you just told me you don't smoke anymore," she said. "I don't. I'm not going there to cop (purchase) any drugs. I need to see this sister. She lives on Sheldon Street," I told her.

Debbie took me to Sheldon Street but parked away from the house I was going to. "What are you going over to that house for? That woman is saved," she said. "I know. That's why I need to see her. She's going to help me," I said.

I got out of Debbie's car. And wouldn't you know - the first person I saw was the dealer I purchased my drugs from. "What's up, Hattie? I got that sho' nuff!" he said. I turned and looked at him. I walked over to him and I said, "I'm going to rehab." He said, "Are you serious? Well, that's straight! I'm glad for you! You have too much sense to waste it out here. I've got much love for you and I hope it works." I said, "It will. The rehab I'm going to is God."

I walked off with my head up and tears rolling down my face. Something was definitely different. I didn't have that deep, dark, empty feeling on the inside, anymore.

# Chapter 14

## *Walking By Faith*

I felt happy. I felt that I was going to be okay. I felt as though it was going to be different this time. Much different than all the others. I believed that everything I'd surrendered to the Lord, that night on the porch, was no longer my burden. I felt lighter. I felt complete. I felt like I was no longer missing anything from my life. I felt as if what I'd been looking for all these years had finally been found. I no longer had to live my life as an addict. I did have a purpose on earth. I had to tell others about the hurt and pain I'd gone through, about the hurt and pain I'd caused. I had to tell people here on this earth. I had to tell them I had looked for love in all the wrong places. Tell them that after looking for 17 years in the places I thought it to be found - it was only found when I surrendered it all - everything, including my wretched life. Surrendered it to the Lord, Jesus. It was then that I found what I was looking for. . . . Deliverance.

I needed to tell people, here on this earth, that they were not alone in their addictions. That there were others out there who had gone through similar trials and could help by encouraging one another. If we believed then we could receive.

As I walked up the sidewalk to that sister's house, fear was taking over. I rang the doorbell. "Maybe what I'm feeling isn't what I'm really feeling." I rang the doorbell again. Bouncing from one foot to the other. Debbie was sitting in her car, watching.

Just as I was about to give up - but not wanting to leave - the sister came to the door. She opened the door, smiling the biggest, prettiest smile anyone had ever given me. She gave me a hug and welcomed me in. There was another sister sitting in the chair. She stood and hugged me, too. I tried not to cry. I just stood there.

Finally, I said, "I want to go to church with you tomorrow but I have no shoes." It was a lie. I did have shoes, they just happened to be the kind you'd wear while dancing on a pole. I didn't know what else to say. She looked at me and smiled that smile. She walked me into her bedroom and told me to pick a pair that I liked. She then said, "Let's have prayer before you go." That was the best thing that ever happened to me.

A horn blew outside. She asked if I had someone waiting for me. I told her no. It was Debbie. She told Debbie, "You can go ahead if you like but Hattie's staying. You're more than welcome to come in and join us." Debbie pulled off.

I remember the three of us forming a circle, while this sister prayed to the Lord. She was praying for God to direct my steps as well as my thoughts. She prayed that I would now lean and depend on His help in everything I did, that from henceforth my past was my past - never to be used or brought up to me again, for bad. That I believed He was my Lord and Savior - My strength. That I no longer had to fight my own battles. He, the Lord would do that for me. This we believed.

That night of February 23, 2004, I accepted the Lord, God as my Savior. It was the best decision I'd ever made.

After that night, I was clean and sober. I had a brand new house to call my own. I had my children with me and began training them up in the way that they should go - so that when they got older, they would not depart.

It was that day, the day that I received God, that I understood I'd have to tell everyone I met about my God and his plan and promise.

# CHAPTER 15

## *My Daily Deliverance*

It's been about four years and I'm still moving forward. I'm not going to tell you that everyday has been easy. I can tell you that every day spent in the Lord God is a good day!

As I look back at my first 30 days of being clean and sober, I realize I was terrified. If I went to the store, I would go two to three blocks out of the way just to avoid anyone. I wouldn't answer the phone. I took my children everywhere I went.

I came to realize that I had to believe the things that I and others had prayed over me. I had to believe the word of God - who is my higher power. So, I stopped walking the long way around. When I saw people, I waved. If I was approached I'd say, "I'm sorry. I don't get down like that anymore. May God bless you."

After a month or two they stopped staring. Some started addressing me as Ms. Hattie or Sister Hattie. I couldn't believe it. I was being respected (because of the Lord!). I enjoyed it. It was because of God, I could now walk down those same streets I once walked down high - with my head up.

I must say that this battle is never over. Only physical death can end it. And now what? Every day is a battle of some sort. I have learned that the battle can be won, if you give it to the right warrior - Christ, Jesus.

My daily life consists of staying busy and encouraging others around me, as well as myself. Daily devotion is a needed tool in my life. I hang around positive people. I try to be pleasing and loving to others, no matter what (to me, this a hard, yet accomplishable task).

I pray continuously throughout the day. This helps to keep my thoughts in the right direction - forward and positive.

I now think about the consequences my actions will have, before I do them.

My most favorable strength is to know that I am a conqueror through Christ Jesus, who strengthens me. He does this daily. Not just once a day, but all throughout the day.

This is how I, Sister Hattie Laws, can make it through each day and know that I am truly delivered.

Lean not unto thy own understanding. Lean and depend on God!

# E P I L O G U E

Dear reader: I am a living witness that the Lord is true to his word. (Hebrew 13:5) says: *"I will never leave thee, nor forsake thee."* In what seemed to be my darkness hour, when I reached out to him, he was there. When I made the wrong decisions, He put me on the right path. When I felt love didnt exist, He loved on me. When I believed that there was no hope, He delivered me.

No matter where you are, no matter whom you are, He's a God that will bring you out of any circumstance if you just trust and have confidence in Him. Remember, He was there through it all with me and He's there for you. Just try Him and see.

Be Blessed.

www.ingramcontent.com/pod-product-compliance
Lightning Source LLC
LaVergne TN
LVHW051647080=26
835511LV00016B/2546